Extra-Terrestrial Contact & Cultural Competency

A field guide for effective communication with off-world visitors

JACK HEART

DEDICATION

This monograph is dedicated to those among us who dare to ask the big questions: "are we alone in the vastness of universe?" What are our true origins as a species? Were we contacted by "others" in the prehistoric past? Are they among us now? Welcome to the world of *High Weirdness* and other such strange occurrences. As we know…
…the truth is out there.

CONTENTS

ACKNOWLEDGMENTS

In compiling this monograph, the author wishes to acknowledge pioneering works of J. Allen Hynek, Jacques Vallée… as well the fertile imaginations of such authors as Douglas Adams. Their foundational contributions to the intriguing topic of UFOlogy, in both fact and fiction, have been foundational in our understanding of that most-mysterious alien entity known as… "the other."

.

1 - INHAPITED WORLDS

"It is known that there are an infinite number of worlds, simply because there is an infinite amount of space for them. However, not every one of them is inhabited. Therefore, there must be a finite number of inhabited worlds.

Any finite number divided by infinity is as near to nothing as makes no odds, so the average population of all the planets in the Universe can be said to be zero. From this it follows that the population of the whole Universe is also zero...

and that any people you may meet from time to time are merely the products of a deranged imagination."

- Douglas Adams

Investigations into Extra-Terrestrial Phenomena and encounters with entities from other worlds/realities, has consistently been an integral component of humanity's interaction with Universe. Throughout recorded history, accounts of contact with Gods, Angels, Demons, Star Beings, etc. are found in all cultures, worldwide. Over time, human understanding of whom or what these phenomena are... has evolved in sophistication.

Hence, ancient mythologies of "egrĕgoroi" or watchers, transform into alien overlords. Old World "fairy folk" evolve into contemporary mythologies of "grey aliens." Small, green-clad leprechauns of centuries past become almond-eyed, "little green men" of the 20th Century. Chariots of the Gods become flying saucers. The boon of the captured leprechaun's pot of gold, transform into transistorized technological marvel, reverse-engineered from crashed saucers.

Contact may take many forms, including but not limited to... physical, archetypical, dreamtime, psychic, trans-dimensional, psychedelic, symbiotic, etc. In considering such phenomena, the prudent investigator would do well to keep options open, so although one might favor an Extra-Dimensional mythology, one should assume, in the interest of comprehensiveness, that all of the above options are equally viable.

Find below select information on the multifarious understandings of extra-terrestrial contact, as well as other noteworthy transmissions & excerpts on this most intriguing topic...

Introduction

This guide is intended to serve as a general briefing to enhance cultural competence while providing insight into the complexities of extra-terrestrial (ET) first contact. Within the context of this field guide, cultural competence is defined as: *the ability to function effectively in the context of planetary cultural differences.* A more specific orientation or training must be provided to individuals, such as diplomatic personnel and social service providers, who will be having repeated or prolonged contact.

First contactees should use this guide to ensure the following *Five Elements of Cultural Competence** are being addressed:

1. Awareness, acceptance and valuing of cultural differences.

2. Awareness of one's own culture and values.

3. Understanding the range of dynamics that result from the interaction between entities of different cultures.

4. Developing cultural knowledge of the particular entity encountered or accessing cultural brokers who may have that knowledge.

5. Ability to adapt individual understanding and communication strategies to fit the cultural context of the individual entity, species, or home world.

*Adapted from Cross, T., Bazron, B., Dennis, K., and Isaacs, M. (1989). Towards A Culturally Competent System of Care Volume I. Washington, D.C.: Georgetown University Child Development Center, CASSP Technical Assistance Center.

2 - LEVELS OF CONTACT

Close Encounter Classifications:
The Hynek Scale

A close encounter is an event in which a person witnesses an unidentified flying object. The terminology and system of classification behind the close encounter was originally developed by astronomer and UFO researcher J. Allen Hynek. This scale was first suggested in his 1972 book: "*The UFO Experience - A Scientific Inquiry.*" Hynek developed his scale in the years following his work with the U.S. Air Force and "Project Blue Book." In developing this system, Hynek's conscious intent was to bring a scientific rigor to the study of UFOlogy. In this scale, the close encounter event is further defined as being one of three distinct sub-classifications...

First - A sighting of one or more unidentified flying objects:

• Flying saucers

• Odd lights or orbs

• Aerial objects that are not attributable to known human technology

Second - An observation of a UFO, and associated physical effects from the UFO, including:

• Heat or radiation

• Damage to terrain

• Crop circles

• Human paralysis (Catalepsy)

• Frightened animals

• Interference with engines or TV or radio reception.

• Lost time: a gap in one's memory associated with a UFO encounter.

Third - An observation of what Hynek terms "animate beings" observed in association with a UFO sighting. Hynek deliberately chose the somewhat vague term "animate beings" to describe beings associated with UFOs without making any unfounded assumptions regarding the beings' origins or nature. Hynek did not necessarily regard these beings as "extra-terrestrials" or "alien" as the close encounter may be one of "ultra-terrestrial" origin. Additionally, Hynek further expressed discomfort with such reports, but felt a scientific obligation to include them, at the very least because they represented a sizable minority of claimed UFO encounters.

Communication Styles:

Nonverbal Messages

• ETs communicate a great deal through non-verbal gestures. Careful observation is necessary to avoid mis-interpretation of non-verbal behavior.

• ETs may look down to show respect or deference to elders, or ignoring an individual to show disagreement or displeasure.

• A gentle handshake is often seen as a sign of respect, not weakness.

Storytelling

Getting messages across through telling a story (traditional teachings and personal stories) is very common and sometimes in contrast with the "get to the point" frame of mind in (western) earthling society. Patience, acceptance and thoughtfulness are critical in establishing and maintaining effective communication. The stories told, often will contain allegorical significance. They will, through the means told, provide critical insight into the nuances of the entities in question.

Myths & Facts

Myth: ETs are inherently spiritual and live in harmony with universe.

Fact: The idea of all ET having a mystical spirituality is a broad generalization. This romantic stereotype can be just as damaging as other more negative stereotypes and impairs one's ability to communicate to ETs as "real people."

Myth: ETs have distinguishing physical characteristics and you can identify them by how they look.

Fact: Due to galactic diversity, as well as thousands of years of inter-world and inter-species interaction, there is no single distinguishing "look" for ETs. Again, this is stereotypical and could lead to unintended consequences in communication.

Self-Awareness & Etiquette

Prior to making contact, examine your own belief system about ETs, related to social issues such as species phobia, mammalian-centrism, terran-centrism and psychedelic drug use, as well as galactic issues such as the potential break-down of consensual reality and the resulting trauma associated with it. You are being observed at all times, so avoid making assumptions and be conscious that you are laying the groundwork for others to follow.

Adapt your thought patterns, as well as your tone of voice, volume, and speed of speech patterns... to that of specific entities... so as to fit their manner of communication style. Preferred body language, posture, and concept of personal space depend on species norms and the nature of the personal relationship. Observe others and allow them to create the space and initiate or ask for any physical contact.

As you establish communication, you may experience expressions of mistrust, frustration, or disappointment, driven by other situations that are outside of your control. Learn not to take it personally. If ETs tease you, understand that this can indicate rapport-building and may be a form of guidance or an indirect way of correcting inappropriate behavior. You will be more easily accepted and forgiven for mistakes if you can learn to laugh at yourself and listen to lessons being brought to you through humor.

Rapport and trust do not come easily in a limited amount of time; however, don't be surprised if ETs speak to you about highly charged issues (e.g., sexual customs and reproductive modalities) as you may be perceived as an objective expert. Issues around gender roles can vary significantly in various ET communities. Common behaviors for humans to be aware of as they relate to gender issues are: eye contact, style of dress, physical touch, personal space, decision making and the influence of male and/or female elders.

For bi-gender species, males and females typically have very distinct social rules for behavior in every day interactions and in ceremonies. Multiple-gender species bring up unique cultural challenges. Not all gender classifications are immediately evident, when coming into contact with ET entities. Careful observation and seeking guidance from an entity elder on appropriate gender-specific behavior can help contactees to follow specific customs and demonstrate cultural respect.

3 - ENTHEOGENIC CONTACT

"I am old, older than thought in your species, which is itself fifty times older than your history. Though I have been on earth for ages I am from the stars. My home is no one planet, for many worlds scattered through the shining disc of the galaxy have conditions which allow my spores an opportunity for life."

- the McKenna Brothers

Interstellar seeding of Intelligent Life

As the discerning reader of this monograph surely knows, Terence McKenna (November 16, 1946 – April 3, 2000), was a ethnobotanist, mystic, psychonaut, lecturer, author, and advocate for the responsible use of naturally occurring psychedelic plants. McKenna was instrumental in developing the *"stoned ape"* theory of the evolution of human intelligence.

He also championed a "novel" extra-terrestrial contact hypothesis. In a psychedelic version of biophysicist Francis Crick's hypothesis of *Directed Panspermia...* McKenna proposed the idea that psilocybin mushrooms may be a species of high intelligence, which may have arrived on this planet as spores migrating through space. Caught in earth's gravitation, these spores landed, germinated, and established a symbiotic relationship with human beings.

In book one of the Tek-Gnostics trilogy, we outline this theory in greater detail. In this monograph, we have re-written and re-arranged elements of that book, to concisely outline psychedelia as extra-terrestrial contact, beginning with a historical perspective. To wit...

The modern era of Extra-terrestrial contact, began during World War II. During the war, fighter pilots began filing reports of strange flying balls of light that often accompanied allied and axis fighter and bomber planes. These aberrations became known as *"Foo Fighters."* Although many strange lights have been reported throughout history, the *Foo Fighters* of WW II and the subsequent UFO/flying saucer phenomena of the 1950's abruptly modernized these ancient flying disc mythologies.

This innovative world view would forever put to rest the angels and demons of old. The emerging modern myth would replace superstitious old-world folktales of the fairy folk with... something new. Old Earth's "Leprechauns" were about to meet the "Little Green Men."

Post World War II, the number of sightings has gone from hundreds to thousands to hundreds of thousands of instances. The mythology has fleshed itself out with subthemes, such as the theme of abduction, or the theme of telepathic contact. It has since become much more difficult to fit all the known facts into the simple model of space-faring visitors from another world. The true origins of extra-terrestrial intelligence on earth may be far stranger... far more unfathomable and fantastic than some metal hulled ship... careening through space.

We have since come to entertain a number of more exotically competing theories in the so-called postmodern phase of thinking about the UFO. Such theories take extra-terrestrial contact beyond a physical handshake. This brings us to the question of the inter-stellar "seeding" of intelligent life.

The late author and lecturer, Terence McKenna contributed a distinctly psychedelic take on the theory of *Panspermia* (the theory that life in the universe is distributed by meteors and asteroids). McKenna believed that mushroom spores were able to survive the vacuum of space travel to become an entheogenic catalyst of human evolution. McKenna's hypothesis brings us to a psychedelic variation on the biological inter-stellar migration theory.

A fungus is a member of a large group of eukaryotic organisms that includes our species class of interest, the noble mushroom. The mushroom reproduces via the dispersal of microscopic spores, capable of surviving for extended periods of time in extremely unfavorable conditions. The following is an excerpt from a McKenna lecture on the subject of extra-terrestrial life:

"My candidate for that kind of an intrusive extra-terrestrial would probably be a mushroom of some sort, or a spore-bearing life form, because spores are very impervious to low temperatures and high radiation... the kind of environment met with in outer space. There's no question that through what's called Brownian motion, which is sort of random percolation, spores do reach the outer edge of our atmosphere, and there, in the presence of cosmic rays and meteors and rare, highly energetic events, occasionally a very small percentage of these biological objects are wafted into space. We even possess meteorites that are believed to be pieces of the Martian surface, thrown out by impacts on the Martian surface of asteroidal material.

In fact I think part of the grappling with the (extra-terrestrial) mystery is going to lead to the conclusion that space is not an impermeable and insurmountable barrier to biology... that in fact planets are islands, and life does occasionally wash in from distant places, and if conditions are correct, can take hold. However, let me say we are dealing, not simply with the phenomenon of extraterrestrial biology, but with the phenomenon of extra-terrestrial intelligence, and this is a hackle-raising notion."

Again, as the discerning reader may know, certain species of mushroom commonly referred to as *'Magic Mushrooms'* when ingested, have a remarkable, psychedelic effect on the nervous system of humans. This effect is characterized by hallucinogenic perception, often revelatory and insightful in nature. This psychedelic experience is so profound, it is often considered to be a form of communication between the ingested mushroom and the human host. Communication infers intelligent interaction between two sentient entities.

Let us explore the "novel" concept of human interaction with an intelligent spore-bearing life form, what we will call the *Magic Mushroom Theory*, in greater detail...

The crux of the Magic Mushroom Theory is that the psychoactive effect of specific mushrooms on the human nervous system constitutes a form of communication between species. It presumes that communication denotes intelligence, and is a form of cognizance and consciousness. This intelligence is in a state of suspended animation during the mushroom's spore phase. It becomes potentially highly active and accessible, via ingestion by a human, during the mushroom's growth and maturity phase. Here is the mythology...

An alien mushroom spore in a state of suspended animation, drifting in space, is caught in Earth's atmosphere. It floats to the surface of the planet, where, under the right conditions, it germinates (possibly mutates) and grows into a mushroom. An unsuspecting earthling hominid finds and eats the mushroom. As it is digested, the mushroom's reanimated psycho-active properties course through the earthling's bloodstream, ultimately reaching the brain. As the psycho-active properties take effect... **"Contact."**

This is a symbiotic relationship. The alien symbiont... or mushroom... requires an interface with a biological nervous system, in order to access and activate its consciousness. It also requires a nervous system's perceptive and motor function capabilities in order to perceive and manipulate its new, three dimensional environment. In other words, the mushroom needs a body to move around in, a brain to "think" in, and eyes with which to see.

Once it enters into a symbiotic relationship with our earthling, it is free to interact and explore in this strange new world, by co-operating or sharing the host's body.

In return, upon entering into symbiosis via ingestion, the earthling host gains access to the mushroom's molecular data-base. Both entities now have access to this data. The information that is transmitted to the earthling takes the form of revelation and insight... thereby increasing the earthling's knowledge base and subsequent intelligence. In this simplistic example, the alien intelligence (that is the mushroom) makes contact with humanoid earthlings in a mutually advantageous, win-win, close encounter. No spacecraft necessary.

Mushroom spores from outer space are, de facto, extra-terrestrial. For purposes of taking our "Magic Mushroom Theory" to its extreme: humanity's discovery and ingestion of the magic fruit of the spore is the close encounter... is contact... with alien life. Accordingly, humanity's explosion of intelligence may very well have been driven by the revelatory and insightful nature of the effect that magic mushrooms have on the human nervous system."

- The Tek-Gnostics Heresies

Entheogenic Cultural Competency

In keeping with the intent of this field guide, we will now outline the protocols of diplomacy, from the mythological perspective of interaction with a psychoactive entheogen, as extra-terrestrial first contact. These protocols assume our psychoactive experience to be a communication with a species of intelligence, vastly older and far stranger than us. A species who has traversed the boundaries of intergalactic space, perhaps for millions of years.

Preparation is key for achieving a culturally competent first contact, under entheogenic conditions. Take great care in selecting an appropriate "setting" where diplomatic relations will occur. The environment should be relaxing, comfortable, and able to accommodate an ambassadorial session of up to 8 hours. Remember... your comfort equates to the eukaryotic ambassador's comfort.

A comfortable setting, complete with bed and blankets, lavatory accommodations, snacks (fresh fruit and tasty beverages), and soothing music, insure a successful first contact. Easy access to natural surroundings, such as ocean beaches or mountain meadows is preferable, but not mandatory. Personal comfort is the main consideration.

In terms of preparation, equal in importance to your setting, is your mindset or "set." As a representative of humanity, your frame of mind is essential to successful diplomacy. A calm, centered state of mind is beneficial in the transition to contact.

It is advised to establish a pre-determined attitude or purpose toward the effect of your thoughts, actions or conduct during first contact. Such clear forethought has been described as *Intention.* Establishing intention represents your commitment to carrying out your actions… as intended.

In setting your intent, be mindful that you are about to be in communication with a species of intelligence, vastly older and far stranger than you. As indicated in the above section on etiquette, approach contact with a sense of humor. This will keep diplomacy "light" and will build "rapport" with the eukaryotic ambassador.

It will become excruciatingly clear when first contact communication begins in earnest. As this form of contact involves other than a physical handshake, you may wish to recline or lay down during diplomacy. You may wish to close your eyes during "the peak" of the session. This is not considered impolite, and may enhance the session.

Physiological and perceptual changes will become apparent as diplomacy gets underway. Eyes often dilate and heart-rate may increase slightly. However, the most striking change is psychological. Expect a distinct gnosis-like quality, which includes a full range of mystical or religious experiential phenomena.

Be prepared that first contact will contain information of an allegorical nature. Through metaphor and/or symbolic transmission, a deeper, meaningful interaction will develop.

Communication may provide significant insight into the nuances of the entity in question, and oneself.

While the most profound interspecies diplomacy will last ninety minutes to two hours... a euphoric after-effect may linger for several hours. This informal time is best spent enjoying the perceptual interactions... enjoying the favor of the snacks and beverages... or exploring the surrounding natural environment.

In the days that follow, processing the experience of first contact may promote complex revelatory insights into the nature of existence... typically accompanied by a sense of certainty that this knowledge is ultimately more relevant and "real" than the perceptions and beliefs we share in everyday life. Again, such is the experience of communicating with a species of intelligence, vastly older and far stranger than us. A species who has traversed the boundaries of intergalactic space, perhaps for millions of years.

4 - EXTRA-DIMENSIONAL CONTACT

"If they are not an advanced race from the future, are we dealing instead with a parallel universe? Another dimension where there are other human races living, and where we may go at our expense, never to return to the present? From that mysterious universe, are higher beings projecting objects that can materialize and dematerialize at will?"

"Are UFOs windows rather than objects?"

- Jacques Vallée

Extra-Dimensional Hypothesis (or inter-dimensional hypothesis) is an idea advanced by Ufologists such as Jacques Vallée, suggesting that unidentified flying objects (UFOs) and related phenomena involve visitations from other realities or dimensions, as opposed to distant star systems within our galaxy. These separate realities coexist (relatively) independent of our "indigenous" reality, yet are extra-dimensionally interlaced with our local reality. Visitors from such other realities, may possess the ability to travel dimensionally versus spatially to our indigenous reality. The Extra-Dimensional Hypothesis (EDH) is an alternative to the extra-terrestrial

Hypothesis.

Many UFO proponents have accepted EDH because the vast distance between stars makes interstellar travel highly improbable using conventional means. Given our temporal constraints... and absent any viable faster-than-light hypothesis... travel between stars utilizing a metal-hulled spacecraft appears to be, from our current technological perspective, an insurmountable obstacle. Within the EDH, it is not requisite to explain any interstellar propulsion method, as it holds that UFOs are not necessarily spacecraft, but rather **Extra-Dimensional-Craft,** or devices that travel between different realities.

One advantage of this hypothesis, as proffered by Hilary Evans, is that it conveniently explains the apparent ability of UFOs to appear and disappear from sight and radar, as reported by a myriad of witnesses, including military and air force personnel. This phenomena is explained as the perceived UFO (Extra-Dimensional-Craft) entering and leaving (materializing and dematerializing) our local dimension. Moreover, Evans argues that if the other dimension is slightly more advanced than ours, or is our own future, this would explain the UFOs' tendency to represent near future technologies (airships in the 1890s, rockets and supersonic travel in the 1940s, etc.).

The Extra-Dimensional Hypothesis also holds that UFOs are a modern manifestation of a phenomenon that has occurred throughout recorded human history, which in prior ages were ascribed to mythological or supernatural events or creatures...

"We are dealing with a yet unrecognized level of consciousness, independent of man but closely linked to the earth.... I do not believe anymore that UFOs are simply the spacecraft of some race of extraterrestrial visitors. This notion is too simplistic to explain their appearance, the frequency of their manifestations through recorded history, and the structure

of the information exchanged with them during contact."

- Jacques Vallée

As we have indicated above, *Extra Dimensional Hypothesis* is a theory suggesting that unidentified flying objects and related phenomena involve visitations from other realities or dimensions. These separate realities coexist independent of our "indigenous" reality, yet are extra-dimensionally or perhaps psychedelically interlaced with our local reality.

In the companion monograph to this volume, titled: *"Return of the Archons – Investigations into the High Weirdness of Alien Intrusion and the Indigenous Mind"* ...we go into great detail in examining the Biblical era Gnostic interpretation of extra-terrestrial entities, known to these archaic mystics as Archons. The ancient Gnostic mythology blurs the line between overt, worldly interpretation of extra-terrestrial contact, and a covert, spiritual understanding of occult, aetheric entities, impacting humanity.

Interestingly, within contemporary esoteric investigations into the ancient Gnostic writings that were uncovered near the Egyptian town of Nag Hammadi in 1945, known as the *Nag Hammadi Codices,* a strange narrative emerged, correlating the Gnostic understanding of the Archons with Ancient Astronaut Theory, extra-terrestrial contact and modern UFOlogy.

Accordingly, the following Abduction scenario has been adapted from these ancient Gnostic materials discovered within the Nag Hammadi Library. The resemblance to entheogenic or psychedelic experiences as well as contemporary reports of close encounters of the third kind is undeniable. ...an induced state of mortal panic, intense feelings of imminent danger or possible abduction (*"take away souls by theft"* – see below). These details present a striking similarity to contemporary ET/UFO lore.

Extra-Dimensional or Psychedelic Abduction Criteria

Translated from the ancient Gnostic text: "Whenever you are seized and you undergo mortal fear, perceived entities may turn on you, thinking they can capture you. And in particular, three entities will seize you… those who pose as toll collectors. Not only do they demand toll, but they take away souls by theft.

Now, when you come under their power, one of them, who is the overseer, will say to you: *"Who are you, and where are you from?"*

You are then to say to him: *"I am a child of humanity and I am from the Source."*

He will then say to you: *"What sort of child are you, and to what Source do you belong?"*

You are to say to him: *"I am from the pre-existent Source, and I am the offspring of the Source."*

Then he will say to you: *"Why were you sent out from the Source?"*

Then you are to say to him: *"I came from the Pre-existent One so that I might behold those of my kind and those who are alien."*

And he will say to you: *"What are these alien beings?"*

You are to say to him: *"They are not entirely alien, for they are from the Fallen Sophia, the female divinity (Mother Earth) who produced them when she brought the human race down from the Source, the realm of the Pre-Existent One. So they are not entirely alien, but they are our kin. They are indeed so because she who is their matrix, Sophia, is from the Source. At the same time they are alien because Sophia did not combine with her like in the Source (her divine male counterpart), when she produced them."*

When he also says to you: *"Where will you go now?"*

You are to say to him: *"To the place when I came, the Source, there shall I return."*

And if you respond in this manner, you will escape their attacks.

- (NHC V, 3. 33 - 34: 1- 25. Translation from NHLE 1990, pp. 265-6 and Kurt Rudolf, Gnosis, p. 174-5.).

5 UFO ETHNOGRAPHY

Ethnography eth·nog·ra·phy (eth-ˈnä-grə-fē) - *noun*
- from Greek ἔθνος ethnos "folk, people, nation" and γράφω grapho "I write" 1) the study and systematic recording of human cultures; 2) a descriptive work produced from such research.

A true *Cultural Ethnography* cannot be achieved in any given social group without a complete emersion into the group in question. This field guide introduces the rudimentary concepts of cultural competency within a classic extra-terrestrial contact scenario. It also introduces the reader to an extra-dimensional contact scenario, adapted from ancient texts. Both scenarios approach the fringes of reason, from different trajectories.

In considering these scenarios, even speculatively, it is important to possess a thorough understanding of the "human equation" within such an encounter. Item 2 of the *Five Elements of Cultural Competence,* found at the beginning of this field guide, stresses the importance of awareness of one's own culture and values. We therefore look to modern UFOlogy and its associated (human) culture.

In fully assessing a cultural ethnography, it is critically important to "know thyself." It is therefore important to possess a working knowledge of the current state of our indigenous, human-centric "Pop" UFO culture. This must be a first-hand, interactive emersion, in order to fully grasp the nuances of said culture.

It was in the spirit of just such a cultural emersion that my esteemed colleague, attorney and personal Guru, Dennis "Agent 87" Igou and I... undertook an odyssey into the strange realm of modern UFOlogy. Over a span of two years, we anticipated, participated, bartered & sold, bystanded & bivouacked in multiple UFO gatherings. Most notably, the History Channel's Ancient Aliens fan event called *"AlienCon,"* and a more immersive affair deep in the Mohave desert, known as *"Contact in the Desert."*

AlienCon was equal parts Ancient Alien presentations and Sci Fi convention, with interesting panels and meet & greet/photo-ops for fans. All the stars one would expect at such a gathering were there. David "Fox Mulder" Duchovny, the star from Fox television's *The X-Files* was there, the granddaddy of Ancient Astronaut Theory, Erich von Däniken was there... and of course the (then) current pop phenomenon, Giorgio A. Tsoukalos (Giorgio! ... Giorgio!) was there. The crowd went wild when Giorgio showed up for his autograph session, I will tell you.

The AlienCon conventions were held in West Coast urban settings. Contact in the Desert on the other hand, was held out in the middle of nowhere, in California's Mohave Desert, near the Joshua Tree National Forest. Joshua Tree, California is approximately 875 due West of Roswell, New Mexico. It is 300 miles due South of the highly classified Air Force facility, infamously known as: Area 51. The alleged events and subsequent notoriety of these two sites have almost single-handedly formed and informed modern American UFOlogy lore.

At "Contact," my associate Agent 87 and I, spoke with or saw speak, the likes of Jacques Vallée, Graham Hancock, Laura Eisenhower and Andrew Collins. We became aware early on that the interests of the various sub-cultures present, expanded well beyond mere ET and AAT theory (or theology), simply because the idea of extra-terrestrial contact cannot be confined to simple, pop-cultural representations.

We recognized a broader understanding of an emerging UFOlogy culture, and consequently broadened our developing UFO Ethnography to accommodate such. We examined the community's deeper, mythic, psychedelic and shamanic aspects, as well as other seemingly disparate topics such as the "New Age" and "Ascension" movements.

One of the most striking realizations to emerge from this odyssey, was the incredibly divergent thought streams present at these events. Consciousness expansion seemed to be the deeper common denominator within the *Contact* experience. The exploration of consciousness had arguably been the central driver of the modern New Age movement, since its inception/revival in the 1960s. The added ingredient at Contact, was an unspoken, perhaps assumed preponderance of psychedelia.

In regard to physical contact... the simplistic notion of meeting an extra-terrestrial face to face... the pop-cultural representation of beings known (within the sub-culture) as: Greys... Reptilians... even Pleiadian space brothers... are too narrow of an understanding of what appears to be going on. Anthropomorphic contact may occur, but our understanding of the phenomena ought not be limited to a physical handshake. Such would be a too simplistic understanding of extra-terrestrial contact.

This experience, whatever it is, unavoidably places us into a conceptual topography that can more accurately be typified as a "psychedelic" experiential realm. This is a topography that literally (and scientifically) defies physiological explanation. Hence contact requires a broader understanding, moving into the realm of the mythic, the shamanic, the archetypical.

Whatever the contact experience is... it likely involves multi-dimensional, plural realities. As indicated earlier, what has been called extra-dimensional hypothesis is an idea advanced by Ufologists (such as Jacques Vallée) who suggest that unidentified flying objects and related phenomena involve visitations from other realities or dimensions, as opposed to distant star systems within our galaxy.

This hypothesis likely involves simultaneous realities... wherein the perceived UFO experience may be <u>both</u> physical and extra-dimensional... at the same time. The UFO may be at once a metal-hulled saucer... and a manifestation of Carl Jung's archetypical mandala... or to use Ezekiel's biblical reference, one that has historically been considered to be a possible UFO encounter... *"Their workmanship looked like a wheel within a wheel."*

Such conceptions move the ET phenomena into the realm of altered states of consciousness. And this, ultimately, is what UFO gatherings, such as the AlienCon and Contact conferences proved to be... a shared, communal willingness to accept multiple streams of thought as to what exactly is happening, when contact with the "other" occurs. Whatever the ET experience is... it defies simple explanation. It moves beyond normalcy into the nether world of High Weirdness. Strange days have found us.

Disclosure & Break-away

A very compelling, recent development within the UFO community is what is commonly referred to as: *"Disclosure."* This brief synopsis is from the Wikipedia group-mind...

"In the early 2000s, the concept of "Disclosure" became increasingly popular in the UFO conspiracy community: that the government had suppressed information on alien contact and full disclosure was needed, and was pursued by activist lobbying groups."

Steven M. Greer... one of the presenters at Contact in the Desert in 2017... has championed this thought-stream since 1993, when he founded the "Disclosure Project," a nonprofit research project whose goal is to disclose to the public the government's alleged knowledge of UFOs, extra-terrestrial intelligence, and advanced, reversed engineered energy and propulsion systems.

For this researcher, one significant point of contention with "pop-disclosure" is that it implies mediation (if not subjugation) of the existence of extra-terrestrial intelligences… to governmental agencies. This does not imply that government entities don't "know things" pertaining to extra-terrestrial contact. Rather, the demand by the public, upon any government for disclosure… implies a level of competency that governments simply do not possess.

Beyond the unsavory implication of conspiracy surrounding disclosure, it is not clear that any governmental body would possess the expertise and wisdom to be an "honest broker" or non-partisan intermediary to extra-terrestrial entities. It is especially doubtful that humanity can rely upon governmental agencies to possess the requisite understanding of what an extra-dimensional encounter might look like.

Universe is a strange & wondrous place and extra-terrestrial contact likely involves forays into extra-dimensional and/or psychedelic realms. A true, deep understanding of such realities is more likely to be found within a shamanic tradition, rather than a scientific or governmental one. Arguably, past government involvement in psychedelia demonstrates a lack of discerning expertise in this field.

In fact, past governmental operations invoke a dark undercurrent of fear and suspicion within the broader UFO community. This fear (& loathing) takes the form of a variety of tales of conspiracy… Operation Paperclip, Mk-Ultra, Chem-trails, Black Ops (& men in black), the governmental cover-up of the existence of extra-terrestrials and the intriguing concept of a covert, break-away plan, instigated by the "powers that be."

With a contemporary suspicion of disclosure, comes the accompanying "Break-away Civilization" conspiracy. This conspiratorial mythology is rooted in Post WWII Nazis, fleeing Europe and taking their secret technologies with them. The so-called Nazi Rat-lines trail to South America and Antarctica, where secret Nazi bases facilitate the scientific development of off-world capabilities. Other developed countries, such as the US, Great Britton and China, following the Nazi lead, develop their own secret space programs.

Thus, the theory goes… there have subsequently been developed, separately or in tandem, a whole "off-the books" civilization… secretly propagated by the PTB, poised to break away from planet Earth.

The world of UFO conspiracy continues to be shaken, with recent revelations, reported by the New York Times. On December 16th, 2017, the Times posted a bizarre breaking news story of an off-the-books, 22 million dollar UFO monitoring program, secretly funded by the pentagon… as well as a black-ops research facility, ran by the private aerospace firm: Bigelow Aerospace. It was reported by the Times that: *"Under Mr. Bigelow's direction, the company modified buildings in Las Vegas for the storage of metal alloys and other materials that Mr. Elizondo and program contractors said had been recovered from unidentified aerial phenomena."*

For the conspiracy minded, this newest revelation demonstrated the government's evolving strategy of secrecy regarding the existence of extra-terrestrial contact. Moving classified operations to a private firm, alleviates the threat of (unsanctioned) disclosure via a Freedom of Information Act (FOIA) filing, submitted by members of the public. A government entity would have to comply with FOIA, while a private firm is not compelled to.

Such conspiratorial angst… be it over Disclosure or Break-away Civilizations… are understandable fears in a world where, what was once considered the wildest of conspiracy theories of the 20th century, proved to be all-too-true in the 21st century. What was once science fiction of the last century, has become dystopian fact in our Brave Noö World. Thus the realm of possibilities continue to expand within UFO communities, world-wide.

In looking back over the 2 years spent in the pursuit of understanding modern UFOlogy, what struck me most, was the sincerity of those intrepid individuals actively involved in examining the UFO phenomena. Those who 87 and I encountered were sincere, honest-to-god seekers of the eternal question: are we alone?

It is for this reason that the UFO sub-culture is so intriguing and endearing. Government conspiracy aside, here is a population asking the big question... Is there intelligent life on other worlds, out there in the vastness of universe? Do they seek us? Should we seek them? Asking the existential question...What is the nature of reality? What is our relationship to "the other" and is the "other" us?

Finally, as indicated at the beginning of this monograph, this field guide is intended to serve as a general briefing to enhance cultural competence while providing insight into the complexities of extra-terrestrial first contact. So too can this guide be used and considered in communicating with other peoples, right here on Earth. Often, it seems that other groups, other tribes appear to come from such a different world-view, such a different perspective... political and otherwise... as to seem foreign, even alien... to our way of thinking.

Consider this guide as a reminder of our cultural differences, as well as our terrestrial commonalities. Let this monograph help define for each of us, a personal world-view... a personal mythology of our place in Universe and act as a guide of competence and integrity, as to how we conduct our interactions with others. At the end of the day, everyone we meet is philosophically considered the "Other" as opposed to the "Self." Besides... can we really be sure that the neighbor watering his or her lawn... right next door... is one of us?

JACK HEART

~ END OF TRANSMISSION ~

28

Field Notes

Field Notes

ABOUT THE AUTHOR

Jack Heart is the proprietor and publisher at Tek-Gnostics Media and creator & curator of tekgnostics.com. Jack is author of *"The Tek-Gnostics Heresies* - *Tales of Wonder from the Collective Conscious"* ...a chronicle of the High Weirdness that is our Brave Noö Future. The Heresies takes a deep dive into the psychedelic nature of Tek-Gnostics, illuminating the system's balance of Artifact & Epiphany.

Raised in the Pacific Northwest, educated on the West Coast, witness to the decline of extractive industries, advocate of environmentally sound transition to a new paradigm... Jack Heart lives with his family at the crossroads of the Siskiyou & Cascade Mountains, in the mythical State of Jefferson.

Jack can most often be found exploring the environs of the Klamath Knot, on the trail of Bigfoot, investigating the anomalies of Mount Shasta & the Oregon Vortex, or relaxing at Stewart Mineral Springs. Jack can be reached at the address provided below...

jackheart@tekgnostics.com